POEMS OF
INSPIRATION

A DAILY DOSE OF
SELF-MOTIVATION

SECOND EDITION

RODRICK WALTERS

Olympus Story House

Contents

Title	Page

Poems of Inspiration: *A Daily Dose of Self-Motivation*
is dedicated to the memory of my cousin and best friend,
Orville James Delano Davis.

You left us way too soon, but even in your absence you still inspire
us to give of ourselves selflessly. We won't let you down.

Rodrick Walters

Acknowledgements

I would like to express my sincere gratitude to the following persons who have been very instrumental in my growth and development. I am forever indebted to you because you've helped me realize and fulfill so many of my dreams. May God continually bless you.

To the members of the Walters family and Davis family – you are too numerous to mention individually but each of you is truly special and I'm so thankful for the family bond that we share.

To my business colleagues – Carole Enisman, Evan Enisman, Maria Barranco and the rest of the team at Premier Wealth Planning and Premier Tax Planning – you embody the term professionalism. It's an honor to know each of you and to call you friends. We've done some great things together; yet there's so much more to do. This journey that we're on is one that will make a lasting impact not only on the economy but also on the lives of those we have the privilege of serving.

To my clients and business associates – serving you and serving with you is a thrill I cannot quite find the right words to describe. The goal is always to add value to you, your lives and your businesses. I hope that this book is yet another "value-add" in our relationship as you continue to pursue your goals.

To my college buddies known as The Posse – Antony Brown, Arthur Edgar, Steve Kendrick, Ejike Okoli, Ike Okoli, Gerald Omari, Edward Rapier – thanks for the brotherhood that we share. We've supported each other through the different phases of life as we've grown from teenage boys with big dreams to what we are now – professionals and family men living out those dreams. Let's keep striving for excellence as we serve others.

To the leaders and members of Word Life Christian Fellowship – it is a true honor to serve the Lord with you as together we seek to make a lasting positive impact on the lives of others.

To my mentors – Audie and Dahlia Anderson, Bishop Arthur and Pastor Beverly Brown, Rev. and Mrs. H. L. Hall, Leo and Fay Martel, Prophet Rohan Rambally, Bishop Courton Reid – you've each made innumerable sacrifices to pour into me so much knowledge and wisdom. You've taught me, led by example and would not allow me to settle for anything less than giving my very best. For this, I am forever indebted to you. As I have received from you, I commit to sharing these invaluable life-changing lessons with others.

To my sister, Sheryl and her husband, Teddy and my nieces, Brianna and Ashley; my brother, Brian and his wife, Karen and my nephews, Kyle and Jaedyn; and my brother, Chris and his wife, Nikki and my niece, Sydney Rose – you all are such an inspiration and encouragement to me in so many ways. Thanks for embracing the values that we have been taught by those who have gone before us. May we ever be mindful of our rich family heritage so that for generations to come, our family will be known for our love for, and our service to, our fellowmen.

To my parents, Terence and Thelma Walters – together you brought me into this world. And although Mom has passed on, the values you have both instilled in me have shaped and molded me and have positioned me to be an agent for change. We come from humble beginnings but the lessons you've taught my siblings and me have lifted us to great heights. May we ever be mindful of the great sacrifices you have made so that we may live our dreams.

To my wife, Dinley, our daughter, Christina and our sons, Nathan and Justin – you inspire me in unimaginable ways. Your unconditional love and support motivate and challenge me to give my all for the betterment of mankind. I could never repay you for the innumerable sacrifices you make so that I can serve others. I trust that you will ever be aware of my gratitude to you. You've brought light into my life and you continue to inspire me more than you will ever know.

And most of all, I thank God, through whom all of this is made possible. You transformed my life in ways that I cannot possibly articulate. You turned my hopelessness and desolation into joy and satisfaction. As You continue to open doors and give me a platform, I commit to You that I will passionately tell others of Your goodness. All glory and honor belong to You.

Rodrick Walters

Introduction

Poems of Inspiration: *A Daily Dose of Self-Motivation* is a collection of poems I have written at different points starting in the late 1990s. The book was first published in 2006 and achieved good success in sharing the message of hope and inspiration. It rose up the charts and was in the top 10 of the new releases in the self-help category on both the Amazon and Barnes and Noble bestseller lists.

So why republish the book? Here's why – since it was first published, certain technological advancements have transformed and revolutionized the way that we communicate. Today, the young and old and everyone in between routinely use tools such as smart phones, tablets and smart watches to communicate, to shop, to read news and so much more.

In addition to this, social media platforms and instant messaging applications have become so commonplace in our daily lives, that the lyrics of the song, *It's a Small World After All* ring true. Messages travel around the world in only a matter of seconds. All these technological advancements have given people the world over – from the simple to the sophisticated – a voice to speak and to let their thoughts be known.

As I have contemplated these great strides that mankind has made since its initial release, I thought that the time was right to reintroduce this book to the global audience. My hope is that the timeless message of inspiration encapsulated within its pages will speak with clarity and purpose to its readers.

The term "inspire" means to stimulate to action or to motivate. Throughout history, people who have achieved greatness seem to have one thing in common—at some point, they became inspired to accomplish what may have seemed impossible to others. They envisioned a different world from many of their contemporaries and had the inspiration to bring to reality what they envisioned. Great scientists, artists, Nobel laureates, world leaders, athletes, and others who have revolutionized the world were inspired to these actions.

The principles shared in this collection of poetry are not new—they have existed throughout all of history. Principles such as goal-setting, positive-thinking, and proactive-planning are timeless and always have proven true when applied with consistency. Regardless of anyone's IQ, education, or socio-economic status, each person is born with the innate ability to think. And those thoughts, as simple as they might seem, can revolutionize lives. Every great accomplishment first began as a thought—and that thought was developed until it grew into something far greater.

I wrote **Poems of Inspiration:** *A Daily Dose of Self-Motivation* to help encourage people to discover and develop their vast potential. It has been my experience that many individuals miss the valuable lessons that life teaches—and in turn live less-fulfilling lives than they truly deserve.

There are thirty one poems in this collection—roughly, one for each day of the month. I strongly urge you to read one per day; this will enable you to absorb the message embodied in each poem. As you reflect on the message—if I have done my job well—you will become empowered to be a high achiever in every area of your life.

The poems address various common issues encountered in the process of becoming successful. Some poems, such as *There's Too Much at Stake* and *No Turning Back*, come from my own experience. Others, such as *Part of the Plan* and *You're Closer Than You Think*, were written to encourage personal friends of mine. *Starting Over* and *A Child in Their Eyes* are fictitious accounts of persons who learned to put into practice the principles of success. *Like a Rocket* is the fictitious account of a musician who rose from poverty, hurt, and disappointment to become a world-famous entertainer.

Like a Beacon is particularly interesting to me because it encourages people who are often awestruck by celebrities, to look within themselves, where they have natural abilities that can make them just as successful or even more successful. *One Day or Day One* is new to this collection of poems yet it is one of the most powerful. It speaks to the tendency that many have – to procrastinate getting started in doing the very thing that will transform their lives into that which they dream about. The message is simple – get started today instead of planning for some ambiguous day in the future.

My desire is that this book will serve as a catalyst for great accomplishments. I hope that as you read, you will see yourself in the person of the poet and embrace the life-changing principles shared in each work; and that in so doing, you will recognize that there are limitless possibilities to what you can accomplish.

Happy reading—your best days are ahead!

Rodrick Walters

S-U-C-C-E-S-S

Start each day with renewed focus

Understand that you have a purpose to fulfill

Count the cost of achieving your purpose

Commit yourself to accomplishing at least one task daily
in order to fulfill your purpose

Expect nothing less than the best possible outcome

Stay true to your convictions

Share your reward with others

The Eagle

If birds of a feather flock together
then why does the eagle roam?
For whether in calm or stormy weather
the eagle flies always alone.

On his own the mighty eagle flies;
he soars to heights unknown.
Alone sees he the vast blue skies;
the world is all his own.

His vision is much sharper than
any other bird of prey's.
From miles away the eagle can
see nature on full display.

The eagle can renew his strength
by changing his feathers and beak.
Instinctively, he knows to shed
the parts that make him weak.

A lesson to humanity
the eagle teaches well.
More than a symbol of liberty,
he has a story to tell.

While others fit in with the crowd,
on your own course embark.
While others sit, you must stand proud
if you wish to make your mark.

With the mighty eagle's vision keen
stay focused on your goal.
For you can realize your dreams—
they're under your control.

When it seems all hope has gone away
and you need your strength renewed,
just like this awesome bird of prey
learn how to start anew.

Then fly above on eagle's wings;
fly on and reach new heights—
for each man has a song to sing
and dreams to put to flight.

There's Too Much at Stake

"Life is a challenge," that's what many say—
a mountain to climb each night and each day.
Sometimes I don't know just how to behave;
there seems no peace, from cradle to grave.

The road less traveled is one full of pain,
of war, and of strife, but what's there to gain?
The road others travel is easy, I see,
but somehow that life has evaded me.

Now here I stand, with foe and with friend,
to walk this road—around each scary bend.
The odds are against me but this path still I choose.
I'll march on ahead—there's nothing to lose.

I've found that it's true, in this life I live,
the struggles I've had have taught me to give;
to reach out to others—the ones who're in need;
to make others smile like captives just freed.

So that is my plight; I accept it with glee—
to live so that blind eyes around me might see.
The road less traveled is the one I must take;
I'll never give up—there's too much at stake.

How Can I Serve Humanity?

Beethoven could write a great symphony.
Sinatra could sing a great melody.
Shakespeare could write a great tragedy,
but nothing great was ever found in me.

In my childhood I read of the great JFK—
how he led our fair nation and showed us the way.
And then I heard of the great MLK
whose dream is still living, even today.

The legend of Florence Nightingale
was not a made-up fairy tale.
Mother Theresa's compassion prevailed;
and who could forget the Princess of Wales?

Well, how can *I* serve humanity?
What shall be *my* legacy?
What greatness could possibly be hiding in me,
that'll ring on through the hallways of eternity?

Tho' my name might not be written in lights
and I might not be onstage with all the spotlights,
in my own humble way I'll serve life with delight,
as I give all I have by day and by night.

The fame and the fortune don't matter to me—
just the service I offer to humanity.
Like great men and great women throughout history,
may my work live for ages, long after me.

The Olympian

I've waited all my life for these next ten seconds.
Getting up early in the morning to train this body of mine.
Preparing it like a well-oiled machine. Denying myself
the pleasures of life—all for this moment.
This is my personal mission.
These beads of sweat dripping down my face
might as well be blood. Because I have given everything
for this moment. I don't even see the people
in the lanes next to me—all I see is that finish line.
I must be the first to reach it.
I refuse to be denied.
Ten seconds is all it will take.
And my life will never be the same.

Follow Your Heart

For so many days life tore you apart;
your hopes and your dreams just doomed from the start.
They said that you learned to make losing an art;
don't listen to them—just follow your heart.

Lonely's the road you walk every day;
the price of success is just too much to pay.
With all odds against you, you can't win this game;
the end, the beginning, it's all just the same.

But listen—you hear it? A beat from within
that says, "You can make it; it's all yours to win."
It speaks words of wisdom wherever you go;
a voice just for you—one that only you know.

Your heart—it'll guide you, in good times and bad;
a friend like no other that you've ever had.
And when you are down for certain defeat,
it gives you the strength to stand on your feet.

You're never alone in this lifelong game;
that beat from within knows you by name.
When hope becomes hopeless, when fortune departs,
just listen within, and follow your heart.

Greatness Within

I've walked all along this lifelong highway;
the lessons I've learned have guided my way.
But I never could solve the deep mystery:
I saw greatness in others, but never in me.

I looked at my father, my brother, my friend;
to life's great heights they always transcend.
Shouldn't I have *his* talents, or *her* dignity?
I can't seem to be happy with just being me.

So I sought and I tried to be like each one,
to get their rewards and to have all their fun.
But strangely I found that I failed every time;
I can't have their gifts—I'll just work on mine.

Could that be the answer? Do I have what it takes?
Could my life make a difference to the whole human race?
Of course, I am gifted, and that's not a sin.
I look in the mirror and see greatness within.

A Chance to Shine

A chance to shine, that's all I ask,
to show the best of me.
It's time to carry out my task,
and play in life's sweet symphony.

So long have I struggled on this road
to walk, to find my way.
But what was once a heavy load
gets lighter by the day.

My journey's not been filled with luck—
the road's been long and tough.
But when some saw a dirty rock,
I saw my diamond in the rough.

I've sweated, labored, toiled, and cried;
I've come through so much pain.
My star just needs a chance to shine;
don't let me wait in vain.

And now a chance is all I need—
won't know if I don't try.
I must complete this masterpiece
before life passes by.

Can't Turn Back Now

It's much too late to turn back now;
I'm almost at my destiny.
I finally found that wonderful sound—
the promise that life has for me.

So long like a child I wandered and roamed—
I wanted to go back home;
I wanted to go to the land of my youth;
the place all my life I have known.

But still there was something within me
saying, "Come to the other side …
Come over, for here the grass is green;
try something you've never tried …"

In walking to my destiny
I learned what I'd never have known;
I learned of the treasures within me—
treasures not known back at home.

My future will be so much brighter
in the land where I long to be;
so now with joy I journey on
to what life meant for me.

I'm almost there, and now I can hear
the sound of an abundance of rain.
I'm way too sure; I can't turn back now—
my life will never be the same.

G-O-A-L-S

Get a clear mental image of what you desire

Organize your thoughts and write them down

Apply yourself to see these thoughts realized

Live as though your life depends on the realization of your dreams

Share what you learn with others

Part of the Plan

You hold down your head, you're feeling so low;
it seems like you never get up off the floor—
for each time you try, you break down and cry;
you look to the heavens and keep asking, "Why?"

"Why do I stumble with each step that I take?
Why do dreams crumble with so much at stake?
Why does it happen again and again—
success is my foe and failure my friend?"

But listen, I tell you—just listen to me—
wherever you stumble, your treasure must be.
The truth of that lesson I've learned in my life:
success is not far from your pain and your strife.

I know it's been hard; I know it's been tough;
the blows that you've taken are more than enough.
And yet you're still standing—you haven't been beat;
I knew that you never could accept defeat.

Now here's your reward: a story to tell
of the struggles you had and the times that you fell.
A story of courage and of victory;
a story to lead you to your destiny.

Make sure that you tell each listening ear
to march on ahead, for there's nothing to fear.
For each time you falter and feel all alone,
that stumbling block is your stepping stone.

So now do you see why you suffered so long?
It's all been designed to make sure you're strong.
So fight on with joy; I'm your biggest fan.
Victory's assured—that's part of the plan.

You're Closer Than You Think

You're closer than you realize
to your date with destiny;
when you will no longer fantasize
about the things you long to see.

You had so many goals and dreams
and plans you talked about.
Ideas like a flowing stream—
you gave no room to doubt.

I know you've wondered many years
if you'd ever see that day.
You've toiled with blood, sweat, and tears
to find only dismay.

The months and years have passed you by;
your stream has seen a drought.
Your passion is about to die—
it seems there's no way out.

But listen: don't you realize
you're closer than you think?
You'll soon see with your very eyes—
you're right now on the brink.

Your night will turn to daylight—
your bad luck into good.
Your dream's about to take flight—
just like you knew it would.

Now do you finally see the light?
The best is yet to come;
for the darkness of the darkest night
must yield to the rising sun.

Sooner or Later

Can't live like this forever—
something has got to change.
To the good life I'm but a stranger;
it always seems out of range.

They told me that sooner or later
there's got to come a day.
They told me that sooner or later
things will go my way.

I've struggled from conception—
my fate, I guess, in life.
Hope seems but deception—
an illusion in the night.

So tired of the darkness,
the struggles in my heart,
the pain, and all the sadness—
I want a brand new start:

a life where I can live
and love and laugh and play;
a life where I just treasure
every moment of the day.

I want the good life sooner;
can't wait for much more time.
Later seems more like forever,
but right now's my time to shine.

My night will turn to daylight,
my bad luck into good,
and my problems into promise—
just like I knew they would.

I choose sooner and not later,
and I'm starting with today.
Now my future's so much brighter—
now the sun will light my way.

Belief in Yourself

I was lost and feeling lonely;
could hardly find my way.
I had no compass to guide me;
my life was in disarray.

Then a friend and true companion
with wisdom I've never known,
shared with me her opinion
of why I was feeling so low.

She said, "You are the one and only
who's ever been made like you.
Be yourself—don't be a phony;
to your own self be true."

That sent me on a journey—
a quest to find myself—
for I couldn't be the real me
while trying to be like someone else.

I'm found that I am gifted
with everything I need.
I'm so glad that burden's lifted;
now life is good indeed.

The lesson learned, I teach you—
you won't be the same again.
Belief in yourself is a virtue
that'll stay with you to the end.

Symphony of Life

Up early another morning
to see the sunrise. The dew rests gently
on the grass after another night. The whisper
of the morning breeze blows sweetly through
the trees. The sparrow flies to greet the day,
like he always does, and
I stroll down by the ocean just to hear
the sound of the waves sailing to the shore.
This makes life worth living.
All creation joins in this daily symphony;
every instrument plays its part.
I must find my role in this;
today is a good day to start.

Won't You Say Yes to Today?

You had a unique vision
of the way that life could be;
you came here on a mission
to help the blind eyes see.

Yet time and trials have caused you
to set your dreams aside;
and now your thoughts frustrate you—
they're always by your side.

Thoughts of your lifelong mission—
your gift to humanity.
They burn in you with passion
and great intensity.

So why don't you release it—
the fire that burns within?
The world around you needs it;
it's time that you begin.

Nothing is as fulfilling
as serving your fellow man;
you're able—are you willing?
Just do it while you can.

So many men have fallen,
but your light will guide their way.
Your destiny is calling—
won't you say yes to today?

Different and Difference

It seems that no matter the places you've been,
somehow you never could seem to fit in.
Like two left shoes, it could clearly be seen
that you always were different—not a part of the team.

"Why is it?" you wondered again and again,
you always seem to be left out in the rain?
While they move with the crowd, you wait there in vain.
While they stand proud, you sit there in pain.

But listen to this: I know where you've been.
Don't look where I am—it's not what it seems.
I've seen many days where I didn't fit in;
how I longed to be free from that burden within.

The truth is your difference just makes you unique.
Don't let them convince you that it makes you weak.
You carry the answers that so many seek.
The lessons you've learned are all yours to teach.

For if everyone was all just the same,
we'd be the same person—just with different names.
Because you are different there's much to attain.
You *can* make a difference—that truth is so plain.

Stand and be proud of who you are,
and let the world see that you are a star.
So let your light shine both near and afar.
The key to life's treasures lies within your heart.

Like a Beacon

How many times have you ever seen
a new celebrity come on the scene?
An actor, a model, an athlete, a star;
someone you admire—if only from afar.

You stand, you applaud, and sometimes you scream;
they're larger than life—or so it would seem.
You gaze at the stars, and what would you give
to walk in their shoes? What a life to live!

But did you ever think of what lies in your soul?
You may be sitting on your *own* pot of gold.
It's time that you know what lies deep down within;
to never find out is almost a sin.

Just look in the mirror—that's where you begin;
you're already a winner—you always have been.
You soon will discover what lies in your heart;
that is the place where your journey will start.

And so shine your light for the whole world to see.
You've got what you need to be all you can be.
Your talents will guide you to soar to new heights,
and be like a beacon that shines in the night.

I'm Changing My Mind

How I got stuck in this rut I cannot explain,
but I'm changing my mind and starting again.
No longer do I want to live in this pain;
another day here will drive me insane.

I'm packing my bags and moving out;
I'm changing addresses—there is no doubt.
I want to learn what life is about.
I'm tired of feeling so down and so out.

My destination is the good life, you see—
the life that has always evaded me.
I've always come close only to be
let down—disappointed, with no victory.

Well today is a new day—it's my time to shine;
yesterday's gone and tomorrow is mine.
I'll live the good life—it's just a matter of time;
there are so many wonderful mountains to climb.

I'm changing my mind—I'm starting today;
this is the day things will go my way.
I'm starting right now—no further delay.
My hope is alive, and it will not decay.

Don't Be Fooled by the Smile that I Wear

Don't be fooled by the smile that I wear,
for each smile you see has cost me a tear.
The fame and the fortune are what you might see,
but let me tell you about the real me:

From birth I have fought just to stay alive.
Despair and doubt have tried to take my life;
no hope, no future, or so it would seem.
Every day to me was like a bad dream.

I lived each day without the comfort of friends;
my broken heart could never seem to mend.
I secretly wondered what would become of me,
because all that I wanted was just to be free.

Well, just when it seemed I was at my wits' end—
when I was ready to be disappointed again,
I stumbled upon a treasure, you see—
a treasure deep down on the inside of me.

I learned I was gifted just like any man—
a gift that's been with me since my life began.
And that gift will always make room for me;
to unlock my treasure, it is the key.

And ever since that wonderful day
just about everything has gone my way.
No longer do I sit and dry my tears—
that is the reason for the smile I wear.

So do not be fooled by the fortune and fame;
the less-traveled road—that's from whence I came.
And if you should look in your heart you will see
a treasure—a gift—to help make you free.

Like a Rocket

He shot like a rocket destined for fame,
but no one was there to feel his pain.
He longed to be loved yet he waited in vain,
till fortune made his a household name.

They sat and they watched him perform on TV—
one of the great entertainers in history.
They danced to his songs: the rhythms, the beats—
the songs that made thousands stand on their feet.

But they didn't see inside the life that he lived:
the price that he paid, all he had to give—
the times he was wronged, yet chose to forgive—
a life that no one else would choose to live.

Because he didn't attend the Ivy League,
some never took him seriously.
Because he didn't hold a degree,
they rejected his every philosophy.

But he learned to live by the ancient truth—
the truth that he learned from the days of his youth:
to love life and live in the daily pursuit
of wisdom and knowledge—life's richest fruits.

And so he rose to fortune and fame
with an easily recognizable name.
So little had he, yet what he became
was a man on a mission, with worldwide acclaim.

The Train

Like a train, this life keeps on rolling;
each day's just a trip down the track.
No stopping on this lifetime journey;
to win, you can never look back.

Your purpose will be your conductor,
to keep all your goals in sight.
To light every part of your railway;
don't look to the left or the right.

Just like the train keeps on moving,
time ticks along like a clock.
You must seize each and every moment
that you hear opportunity knock.

The route ahead is uncertain—
you don't know what lies 'round the bend.
But stay on the right track and don't ever look back—
it'll all work out in the end.

Your train's pulling into the station;
make sure it doesn't pass you by.
Your destiny is waiting.
Get on for the ride of your life!

A Child in Their Eyes

His mom and dad sat amazed and surprised;
he was only a boy, a child in their eyes.
They wondered how he was young but yet so wise.
They asked how he learned the secret to life.

"Remember that summer before Grandpa died?
How I went to his house, and we played outside?
He taught me a lesson that serves as my guide,
and that's why I speak of him with such great pride.

"He said that I only have one life to live,
so I must learn to love and forgive.
He said that my actions will always outlive
the words that I say and the excuses I give.

"He told me the secret of true success:
'Prosperity, peace, and happiness
are not in all of the things we possess,
but in the lives that we touch and the love we express.'

"I promised him that I would strive to be
a young man of high integrity—
to shine my light for the world to see,
and do unto others as I want done to me.

"So that's why I choose to live this way;
my actions speak more than the words I say.
Tomorrow's not promised, so I vow every day
to shine like the stars in their perfect array."

Freedom Is the Cry of Every Man

Freedom is the cry of every man—
a foundation on which to stand.
Freedom to think, to imagine, to be;
freedom brings dreams to reality.

How can the bird fly unless it's free?
Or dreams take flight without eyes to see?
The eyes of the wise are the ones we should cherish,
for when there's no vision, we surely will perish.

A free mind can make a pauper a king
when it discovers the potential deep within.
It marches to the sound of its own unique beat,
and helps make the life of a dreamer complete.

All men should have the liberty
to live their dreams – whatever they may be.
For every man deserves the right
to soar like an eagle to higher heights.

Starting Over

Starting back at square one
isn't an easy thing to do.

She had everything—
her career,
her possessions,
and
the family of her dreams.

Then it seemed like,
all at once,
she lost it all.
The walls came crashing down around her.
But deep down, on the inside,
her heart never missed a beat.

She knew that, somehow,
she'd rise from the ashes in which she lay.

She had lost it all, but yet she rose again—
because hope
never
went
away.

Tomorrow Is Mine

Gone are the ills of yesterday
with all their sorrows and woes;
the promise of a brand new day
gives a hope I never have known.

I struggled so long to find my way
in this long journey of mine.
Now the sad night is o'er; today's a new day,
and now it's my time to shine.

The darkness of night I've known all my life—
it's made hope seem so far away.
But now I can see a light from afar;
my guide—my brand new sun ray.

The lessons I've learned—too many to tell,
have brought me a mighty long way.
My teacher is life, and it has taught me well;
I learned what I learned the hard way.

And now I can see that it all had to be,
or I'd walk the same road every time.
Yesterday's gone—but today I am free,
and I know that tomorrow is mine.

Like Planting a Seed

Impossible is nothing if you only believe;
for whatever you imagine you can achieve.
The greatest success must start with a dream.
The life you desire must first be foreseen.

The road to success is like planting a seed,
and watching that seed become a tree.
You nurture it, protect it, that seed that you have sown,
and when it's grown, it stands tall on its own.

The seed of success must be sown in your mind,
and nurtured, protected with each step you climb.
No matter how strong the winds of life blow,
you will rise above and stand on your own.

So never, my friend, be afraid to dream—
that's the seed that will help you to reign supreme.
So dream your dream, it's all your own;
and with it, I promise, you're never alone.

One Day or Day One

For all of my life, through the struggles, the strife,
through the pain life would send my way,
I hoped and I dreamed that someday I'd succeed;
I would finally make it one day.

I looked at my peers as they conquered their fears
and marched on with faith anyway.
I saw with my eyes as they realized
the rewards on this lifelong highway.

But what about me? Can I ever be free?
'cause it seemed hope had led me astray.
Truths just became lies each time I'd fantasize
about things finally going my way.

Then one day I said, "My dreams are not dead—
no more shall I live in dismay.
I'll make up my mind and leave my worries behind;
new hope is arising today."

I said to myself, "Be true to thyself;
you alone have the right words to say.
You know you can win if you only begin;
don't wait – just get started today!"

No matter the cost, my dreams won't be lost;
I'm like a lion stalking its prey.
One hundred percent, I'll never relent;
my *someday* is starting today.

Today is day one, my new life has begun;
from this path I will never stray.
To this oath I am bound – let the heavens resound
with these words I declare on this day!

No Turning Back

Can't do it any longer; I keep lying to myself.
The yearning and the hunger won't go anywhere else.
It's time to feed my passion; it's time to take control;
it's time to take some action before I get too old.

How can I serve humanity by sitting on the fence?
How can I give the best of me, living with this pretense?
I've got so much inside of me that I've got to let it out.
It's time to give the rest of me, and that's without a doubt.

No more procrastination; I won't die in a cocoon.
And no more contemplation; I've got to do it soon.
Can't live with all the sorrow; can't see my dreams decay;
the fool lives for tomorrow – the wise man for today.

There's a fire on the inside— one that I can't contain—
that's yearning for the outside, where it can have free reign
to lead me to my destiny, to where I long to be,
to burn for me eternally, to make my life complete.

With one look in the mirror, I know I'm on my way;
with each step I get nearer, so I must start today.
The world out there is waiting; it's time to get on track—
this time, no hesitating; there is no turning back.

A Lasting Legacy

May I seek to serve my fellow man,
and give of myself and do all that I can.
May I love and give a helping hand—
that's the foundation on which I stand.

For what is my life if not to live?
And what is my purpose if not to give?
When my life has ended I cannot relive
the moments I now have to love and forgive.

Each day as I awaken and watch the sunrise
and offer my life as a sacrifice,
may I teach all I know, and give good advice—
displaying integrity with no compromise.

Whenever I come to the end of my days
and I go to my final resting place—
when the sun goes down and I finish this race,
may I leave this world a better place.

This is my vow to humanity—
a vow that will last all eternity.
For my children and all who will come after me,
may I leave a lasting legacy.

A-C-T-I-O-N

Acknowledge your strengths and weaknesses

Consider the limitless possibilities of what you may accomplish

Take small steps daily toward realizing your dreams

Inspire others to join you on your journey

Obey your instincts and work relentlessly

Nurture your dream until it becomes reality

www.ingramcontent.com/pod-product-compliance
Lightning Source LLC
Chambersburg PA
CBHW040859120626
46551CB00001B/89